The Snatching of Horrible Harold

A Play for Children

John Gardiner and Fiz Coleman

A Samuel French Acting Edition

SAMUELFRENCH-LONDON.CO.UK
SAMUELFRENCH.COM

Copyright © 1985 by John Gardiner and Felicity Coleman
All Rights Reserved

THE SNATCHING OF HORRIBLE HAROLD is fully protected under the copyright laws of the British Commonwealth, including Canada, the United States of America, and all other countries of the Copyright Union. All rights, including professional and amateur stage productions, recitation, lecturing, public reading, motion picture, radio broadcasting, television and the rights of translation into foreign languages are strictly reserved.

ISBN 978-0-573-05074-9

www.samuelfrench-london.co.uk

www.samuelfrench.com

For Amateur Production Enquiries

UNITED KINGDOM AND WORLD EXCLUDING NORTH AMERICA

plays@SamuelFrench-London.co.uk

020 7255 4302/01

Each title is subject to availability from Samuel French,

depending upon country of performance.

CAUTION: Professional and amateur producers are hereby warned that *THE SNATCHING OF HORRIBLE HAROLD* is subject to a licensing fee. Publication of this play does not imply availability for performance. Both amateurs and professionals considering a production are strongly advised to apply to the appropriate agent before starting rehearsals, advertising, or booking a theatre. A licensing fee must be paid whether the title is presented for charity or gain and whether or not admission is charged.

The professional rights in this play are controlled by Samuel French Ltd, 52 Fitzroy Street, London, W1T 5JR.

No one shall make any changes in this title for the purpose of production. No part of this book may be reproduced, stored in a retrieval system, or transmitted in any form, by any means, now known or yet to be invented, including mechanical, electronic, photocopying, recording, videotaping, or otherwise, without the prior written permission of the publisher. No one shall upload this title, or part of this title, to any social media websites.

The right of John Gardiner and Fiz Coleman to be identified as author of this work has been asserted by them in accordance with Section 77 of the Copyright, Designs and Patents Act 1988

CHARACTERS

Denis, a dustman
Edith, Harold's mother
Mrs Thompson, a neighbour
Horrible Harold, Edith's monstrous offspring
Granny Grot, owner of the Grot Shop
Mr Slickerbotham, owner of the Dry Cleaning
  Emporium
Freda ⎫
Clarissa ⎬ Slickerbotham's assistants
Megagerm, a formless, amoebic germ creature
Archie, Harold's father

Mrs Thompson can double Megagerm

The action takes place in Brick Street and at Mr Slickerbotham's pre-processing laboratory

Act I   Dustbin collection day
Act II The same evening

Description of Characters and their Costumes

Denis. An amiable, easy-going Cockney dustman who works the Brick Street area. In Act I he wears a flat cap, old and battered trousers (which are far too big for him), checked shirt, old stained waistcoat, large boots and a pair of big, dirty, old gloves. In Act II he wears a checked woolly dressing-gown.

Edith. A harassed, worried "mum". Mother of Harold and wife of Archie, she works as tea-lady in Mr Slickerbotham's Dry Cleaning Emporium. In Act I she wears a headscarf, sensible but boring blouse, pleated skirt with her petticoat hanging below the hem, thick, wrinkled stockings, flat shoes or plimsols, flowered wrap-over pinafore, and three-quarter length imitation leather coat. In Act II she requires a bright orange or pink shortie nylon nightie, furry slippers, hair net, rollers and face-pack.

Mrs Thompson is a scruffy housewife wearing a dressing-gown, tatty slippers and with a cigarette hanging out of her mouth.

Horrible Harold. A monstrous offspring who lives in a pram. Son of Edith and Archie he is aged twenty-six but has been mentally stunted since his Dad's disappearance. He wears a knitted blue bonnet, blue matinee jacket, mittens or gloves, bootees, gigantic (suspiciously stained) nappy—a large white bath towel is best—large dirty bib, big dummy on a ribbon, tattoos on arms and spots on face and cheeks.

Granny Grot. The owner of the Amazing Grot Shop, who deals only in grotty, stuffy, old rubbish and gungey things. She is elderly and eccentric. In Act I she wears a straw hat decorated with vegetables, high-necked Victorian white blouse, short, brightly coloured "garibaldi" jacket, finger-less gloves, brightly coloured scarves around neck, voluminous skirt covered with multi-coloured patch pockets, brightly coloured tights or leg-warmers, bloomers, button-up boots, beads, chains, glasses and binoculars hanging around her neck. In Act II she wears a Victorian nightdress, shawl, mop cap or bonnet, with a cloak for the street scene. A satchel-type bag might be useful in Act I for carrying props.

Mr Slickerbotham. The immaculate, evil and shifty owner of the Dry Cleaning Emporium. He wears a white tail suit, white shirt, white bow-tie, white waistcoat, white gloves and white shoes. Do not make-up his face in any way.

Freda and **Clarissa.** Mr Slickerbotham's semi-robotic assistants. Dressed in white all-in-one boiler suits with white motor-cyclist silk helmet inners or balaclavas, white gloves, white plimsols with clown CTV white pancake make-up. For the costume change in Act II either a set of identical but filthy costumes, or net drapes to go over existing costumes from which hang shredded dustbin liners, old foam, string, general gunge with stockings pulled over faces.

Megagerm. A formless conglomeration of germy things. Megagerm should be frightening. His costume is made out of black lining material with strips added to break up his human shape, over the top of some stiffer paper or cardboard which is mis-shapen. His head mask should be twice the size of a human head and a kind of gigantic globule of boils, bumps and pustules. Below this costume he wears a white boiler suit and balaclava for transformation in the Processor. It is essential that on entry Megagerm's feet are hidden and that it appears to float. His movements should be flowing and menacing—nearly slow-motion.

Archie. Harold's long-lost Dad and Edith's long-lost husband. Dressed in either long grandad combinations or singlet vest with very baggy short underpants.

Production Notes

The playing area should be very simple and can either be played on a conventional proscenium arch stage or, as in the original production, played as "theatre in the long" (see set plan on Page 34). The following directions assume that the director has decided to stage his/her production on the floor of the area i.e. hall, room, theatre auditorium. The area is set out as a street, which stretches the length of the space. The audience sit either side of the street, raked, looking down on Brick Street. There is a zebra or pedestrian crossing in the centre of the street, a letter-box and street signs on the walls and any other paraphernalia that the company feels necessary.

At one end of the street is Granny Grot's Grot Shop; there is a door but the interior of the shop and all the grottery is clearly visible to the audience. There is a small area in front of the shop where Harold is later left for his evening nap, but the inside is a complete shambles. There is a counter and many shelves displaying bottles full of coloured water and labelled with bizarre potions: "Essence of Newt", "Nasty bits" and "Tincture of Toe-Clippings", etc. Books, old hats, sinks, gardening tools, a gramophone, a busted piano, jars, junk and jumble are among the things to be found inside.

At the other end of the street is the immaculate exterior of Mr Slickerbotham's Dry Cleaning Emporium. The front façade is clearly visible but for the moment the Processor and other mysteries are hidden from the audience until the sliding door is lifted (see Page 34).

Outside each shop you have a lamp-post on a separate dimmer, as these help to create the sense of night falling in Act II and in the latter part of Act I. These are optional but can be made quite simply with cardboard tubing and ingenuity.

As the Audience arrive, they can be shown to their seats by a variety of street people. For example, Old Sid, the barrel-organ player, policemen, traffic wardens, postman, posh women out shopping, delivery people, flower seller, winkle seller, ice cream vendor, etc. All of these characters can be given specific funny tasks. The traffic warden nicks kids for sitting still too long in one spot; kids help the postman empty the box full of strange objects; delivery men get kids to knock on Slickerbotham's place to deliver a parcel; Mrs Thompson can come out and get it, etc.

When the Audience are settled, the Street People disappear and the street is brilliantly lit as we hear Denis singing offstage.

ACT 1*

The characters in the street (if used) have dispersed and, as the House Lights fade, the street area, Granny Grot's Shop and Mr Slickerbotham's Emporium become brightly lit. The audience is first made aware of Denis the dustman by his singing offstage a snatch of "My Old Man's A Dustman"

Denis (*calling off*) Be wiv you in a tick, Charlie. Just got these bins down Brick Street to do.
Voice (*off*) OK, Den.

Denis enters, singing. He slows down on the last line as he produces a bag of old rubbish or an apple and aims to get it in Granny Grot's dustbin

There is a drum roll and a crash as it goes in

Yeah! (*His arm is aloft like a darts player. He sees the audience*) Mornin', darlin'. (*He shakes hands with the audience*) Wotcher sunshine. (*He shakes hands again*) Bit nippy this morning in' it? Now, what we got down Brick Street today? (*He lifts the lid on Mrs Thompson's bin*) Cor, don't like the look of this one. (*He sniffs and goes cross-eyed*) Phew! Wot a pong!!

Mrs Thompson enters carrying a newspaper and smoking a cigarette

Mrs Thompson All right, Denis, what's wrong now?
Denis Wot's wrong, Mrs Thompson? Wot have you put in your bin? It's disgusting!
Mrs Thompson Cabbages and cat food.
Denis Now she tells me.

Really deafening "heavy metal" music is heard

Mrs Thompson (*shouting*) I know who that'll be. Young 'Arold and his mum, Edith.

The music fades

Denis Poor Edith. Wot a tragical life she's had. Her husband ...
Mrs Thompson (*butting in—she's a know-all*) Archie.
Denis (*looking at Mrs Thompson*) Archie. Pops upstairs one night to tuck young Harold in, tell 'im his horror story and ...
Mrs Thompson (*interrupting*) ... give 'im 'is ham sandwich.
Denis ... give him 'is ham sandwich—when what do you think happens? Well, Archie ...

---

*N.B. Paragraph 3 on page ii of this Acting Edition regarding photocopying and video-recording should be carefully read.

Mrs Thompson (*interrupting again*) Harold's Dad.
Denis Harold's Dad, just disappears. Whoosh! Just like that. One minute he was there ...
Mrs Thompson The next minute he weren't there. All that was left, not a word of a lie, was 'is trousers, 'is boots and 'is shirt. Not a sign of Archie anywhere.
Denis
Mrs Thompson } (*together*) Very mysterical.

Mrs Thompson picks up her morning milk bottle and exits

Denis (*moving to another part of the street*) And he's never been heard of from that day to this. The police were completely baff-boozled. And so there's poor Edith left to bring up the nipper all on her tod. Course it affected Harold summinck chronic—stunted his growth, well, I mean it ain't natural to 'ave yer Dad disappear on yer like that and ...

Mrs Thompson sticks her head out of her door

Mrs Thompson He never got his ham sandwich.
Denis
Mrs Thompson } (*together*) Terrible business.

Heavy metal music is heard again

Edith enters, pushing a large pram containing Harold which is covered with football slogans, Guinness adverts and lots of graffiti like "Harold rules, OK", "Who nicked my Dad?", and "I luv Wally". Smoke is coming from the pram suggesting that Harold is having a cigarette

Denis (*over the din*) Mornin' Edith!
Edith (*flustered*) Mornin' Denis!
Denis Mornin' Harold!
Harold Wotcher Den!
Denis Everyfink OK?
Harold Yeah. Wanna sausage? (*He holds out a big red sausage*)
Denis Er, not just now Harold, thanks.
Harold Good. (*He puts it back inside*)
Denis 'Ere, Edith, you're a bit late for work, ain't cher? (*He looks at his watch*)
Edith I know, Mr Slickerbotham'll kill me. But it's this pram. Pushin' it up that hill and 'Arold's gettin' such a weight these days. (*Louder*) 'Arold, please turn your tranny down a bit, love.

The music fades

Denis That's it Harold. Anyway, *Play School*'s comin' on the tele now.
Harold Goody, goody!

There is activity in the pram, a blue flicker and the opening credits of "Play School" emerge from the interior. Harold laughs. He likes it

Act I

Edith (*moving away to speak to Denis*) Oh, a bit of peace at last. He loves his *Play School*, that and the late night thriller. Honest Denis, he's gettin' to be a real 'andful.

Harold gives a huge guffaw

See what I mean? He's growing so fast. I can't 'ardly keep up with him now his stunted period's ended.

Denis (*laughing*) I bet the old family allowance don't cover his milk bills now.

Edith Milk. M-I-L-K? 'E's on to Guinness now.

We hear a Guinness can being opened, poured and consumed noisily, with a burp?

Harold (*noisily*) Luvly!

Edith Still, he don't have many little treats these days and 'e needs to keep his strength up, now his Dad's gorn and that. (*She sniffs*)

Denis Calm down Edith. Don't take on so. Look, 'ave my hankie. (*He pulls out a filthy dustman's rag*)

Edith (*not sure*) Ohh. Thanks, Den. You're ever so kind and caring.

Denis Think nuffin' of it, Edie. You know I'd do anything for you and 'Arold. That reminds me (*addressing the pram*) 'Arold, look what I've brought you.

Harold Wozzat?

Denis (*to Edith quietly*) Does he like crisps?

Harold (*hearing*) Crispies?

Denis Oooo, I should say he does. Monster Munch is his favourite.

Denis That's what I got 'im.

Harold (*very excitedly*) Monster Munch! Goody, goody!

Edith Oh, lovely Den. (*Speaking very clearly to the pram as to a very small infant*) Look-Harold-from-your-Uncle-Denis. A-lovely-packet-of-Monster-Munch. (*She holds them out*)

Harold's hand comes out and grabs the crisps

Harold Grrmusunchy. Crunncchhhyyy.

Revolting sounds are heard and then almost immediately the empty packet is ejected. Harold blows a siren to accompany all missiles ejected from the pram

Denis Mmm. Blimey. He do like 'is food, don't 'e?

Edith (*dreamily*) Oh yeah. (*She snaps out of her dream*) Anyway, Denis, ta everso, but I gotta get a move on. Mr Slickerbotham'll be wanting his "elevenses" any moment.

Denis Bit early for elevenses innit?

Edith Yes, I know, but he's that particular, he insists on 'avin' is cups and saucers scrubbed spotless and dried three times before 'e'll drink out of 'em.

Denis Three times! Strange.

Edith Peculiar.

Harold (*in a deep voice*) Crackers!
Denis 'Ello. His conversation's comin' along a treat. Clever little lad ain't 'e?
Edith (*laughing*) Oh no, Denis—he means he wants his cream crackers. Here you are, mummy's little angel.

Edith pulls out a packet of cream crackers and gives them to Harold. They meet the same fate as the crisps—an empty packet emerges

Slickerbotham's thin, wheedling, cruel voice is heard off, from his shop

Slickerbotham (*off*) Where is that wretched woman with my tea?
Edith (*freezing*) That's old Slickerbum. I must fly, Denis, before he does his nut.
Denis OK. Bye love. Ta ta, Harold, be a good little boy and help your mum.

Harold blows a raspberry, the cassette player goes on, teddy-bear and other toys, obviously vandalized, Guinness can, etc., are ejected from the pram

Edith wheels him into the Dry Cleaning Emporium

Denis clears up and dumps the rubbish in Granny's bin

Gawd. He's turning into a right handful is that lad. Well, let's get cracking on these bins eh? Never know what you'll find in bins. That's why I like the job. Not that I'll find much in that one. (*He points to and picks up the bin outside Granny's Grot Shop*) This bin belongs to me old mate, Granny Grot. This is 'er place—don't throw nothing out she don't—she's got a use for everything and anything (*pointing to the shop*)—toothless combs, used tea-bags, old toast. She mixes 'em all up in her potions. Yeah, and she takes in special orders for high quality grot. People come from miles ... to buy her stuff. Chinese, Japanese, ... Pekinese—no seriously though, any old stuff I pick up in the bins I know Granny Grott'll find a 'ome for it. She's OK is Granny Grot—bit loony like, but she's got a heart of gold. Not like 'im down the other end (*he moves to Slickerbotham's Shop*) 'Im and 'is "super clean Dry Cleaning Emporium". (*Shouting*) Bloomin' show-off. It ain't fair that poor old Edith has to work for 'im. (*He picks up a bin*) If I had my way I'd stick a dustbin right up his ...

Slickerbotham appears suddenly at his door. He is walking backwards admiring the front of the shop, when Denis accidentally swings the bin up his backside

... Oh! Er, morning Mr Slickerbotham. You got any rubbish for me this week?
Slickerbotham Of course I have. You stupid idiot. It's in the bin (*he indicates*) and don't hang around here afterwards. I don't want filth around my Dry Cleaning Emporium. (*Calling indoors*) Clarissa!
Clarissa (*off*) Beep! (*A vocal electronic sound*)
Slickerbotham Freda!
Freda (*off*) Beep! (*Another vocal electronic sound*)

Act I   5

Slickerbotham Dust inspection and drain polishing.
Freda } *(together, off)* Yes, Mr Slickerbotham. Beep! Beep! Beep!
Clarissa

Slickerbotham goes back inside

Denis See what I mean? Dust inspection! Drain polishing! I ask you.

The sounds of hoovering, polishing and banging are heard inside the shop

Freda *(off)* Scrub.
Clarissa *(off)* Polish.
Freda *(off)* Inspect.
Clarissa *(off)* Disinfect.
Freda } *(off, in unison/robotic)* Yes, Mr Slickerbotham. Immediately Mr
Clarissa   Slickerbotham. Beep! Beep! Beep!
Denis *(imitating their servility)* Yes, Mr Slickerbotham. No, Mr Slickerbotham. Three bins full, Mr Slickerbotham.

Hoover sound fades

That's his two assistants. Finicky Freda and Clean-up Clarissa. *(With emphasis)* I hate 'em both. Yesterday I saw them spraying the windows round the back pure white. They can't abide anything a bit scruffy or dirty. You can't even see inside those windows now. Barmy! 'Ere. *(To the kids in the audience, secretively)* If I was you I'd sit on your hands before Slickerbotham and his assistants come round. They'll inspect your fingernails as sure as potatoes grow and they'll whip 'em orf before you can say "Snipper botham"! Nar, I'm only jokin'. But I tell you what. You could do me a real favour. Would you all keep a look-out for old Slickerbum while a couple of you 'ave a rummage around in his bin? See if you can find any good stuff for Granny Grot. *(He selects a couple of rummagers from the audience)* Now don't forget you hold up all the stuff so's the others can see and then if you think its grotty enough just shout out "GROTTY!" and then you two, put it to one side for old Granny G. Let's do one together, shall we? You've got the idea, Grreat! I'll just nip down and see 'ow Charlie's doin' down the pickle factory. *(He moves, then stops)* In a bit of a pickle I expect. *(He laughs at his awful joke)* See you in 'arf a mo. Remember—GROTTY means GREAT. Good rummagin'.

Denis exits

The two children start to pull things out of bin—if the audience shout out "GROTTY" they put them to one side. The children discover a string of black sausages, a bottle labelled "Damaged Bluebottles", a pair of large black knickers, marked "Freda's", a whoopee cushion and a spokeless umbrella

Slickerbotham enters, stealthily, as they remove the last objects

Slickerbotham What in the name of Harpic is going on here? What are you filthy brats doing inside that revolting receptacle?

Denis enters at a sprint

Denis Sorry, Mr Slobberbotham, er Slickerbotham. It's all my fault. They

was just 'elping me. (*Winking to the kids*) Just helping me out. Keeping the place spick and span. Fancy a pickled onion?
Slickerbotham Disgusting!
Denis (*looking at the onion*) No—maybe you're right.
Slickerbotham (*ignoring Denis and addressing the audience*) Spick and span eh? Good! That's what I like to hear. And what I like to see are nice children with common sense and clean habits. No dirty fingernails, I'll have them off! No filthy tide-marks around the neck. I'll scrub them raw! Now, you! (*He turns to Denis*) Get this muck out of here and away from my shop-front immediately. Clarissa!
Clarissa (*off*) Beep!
Slickerbotham Freda!
Freda (*off*) Beep!
Slickerbotham I hope you are still polishing and purifying!

Slickerbotham exits and the sound of Hoovering is heard as he opens and closes the door

Clarissa ⎫
Freda ⎭ (*together, off*) Yes, Mr Slickerbotham. Beep. Beep! Beep!
Denis Sorry about that. Did you find any good stuff? (*He sees the stuff*) Oh, great grot! Cor, Granny'll go grananas when she sees this lot.

The sounds of a bicycle bell, a motor horn and a train whistle are heard off

'Ello, that sounds like her coming now. Course, it's Tuesday. I 'spect she's been out collecting down the Council tip.

Granny enters on a very old-fashioned bicycle or pushing a wheelbarrow. She is singing the following, very badly, to the tune of "The Sound of Music"

Granny   The tips are alive with the piles of grotty
              The dumps are divine, and my heart's aflame.
              The bins are all bursting with glorious gungey
              As I fly to my Paradise of Pong.

Trailing behind the bicycle on a rope, or in the wheelbarrow, are old saucepans, an old bird-cage, cans, a battered suitcase and general bric-a-brac. Granny is an untidy, bizarre, bohemian character—warm, generous and capable. Her collection of grot is used either to sell for profit or to create a variety of potions and patent medicines. She wears a large hat decorated with broccoli, rhubarb, celery and a stick of liquorice. Her long black patchwork skirt has pockets which contain a bag of Grot-stoppers, "Fleur de Grot" spray and a magic stick. She trails woollen scarves and around her neck is a collection of spectacles and beads, a magnifying glass and a pair of binoculars. Up the leg of her bloomers are a till receipt roll and a small bottle labelled "Grot Tonic"

(*She screeches to a halt and then breathes in the morning air in great gulps*) What-a-beautiful morning! (*To the children*) Just the weather for Grot Grubbing. But first, my morning exercises. (*Ad libbing, she invites the children to join in*) Right. A good cough! Big sniff! Stretch out your arms

Act I

in front of you. Wiggle the fingers. Excellent and now bend down and up, down and up.

Denis joins in but goes up when he should go down

Splendid! Feeling better than ever! (*She finishes the exercises*) Good morning E-v-e-r-y-b-o-d-y! Morning Denis! (*She suddenly stops and sniffs the air and Denis*) Mmmmmm, you smell delicious, Denis. (*Nose twitching*) What is it? "Fleur de Grot"? (*To the audience*) That is one of my best selling potions you know.

Denis Give 'em a dollop or two.
Granny Why not, Denis? (*She pulls out the spray*) Plenty to go round. (*She squirts the audience liberally*) Anyone fancy a "Grot-stopper"?
Denis They're fantastic!
Granny Fantastic—they change colour as you suck 'em and (*holding one up to the light*) there's a Brussel sprout in the middle. (*She pulls out a bag, and passes them round*) Now, stick of celery anyone?—thank you! (*Handing to a child without asking permission*) Stick of rhubarb? You're most kind. Stick of broccoli? Good. Stick of liquorice anyone?
Denis Cor, yes please.
Granny Here we are then Denis . . .

Denis goes to eat it

It's for one of our friends.
Denis Oh yes—corst. (*Disappointed—he hands it to an outstretched hand and whispers*) Save us a bit for later.
Granny Good heavens! How on earth did that get in there? (*It is a small conjurer's stick*) Never mind, a bit of colour never did any harm. (*She places the stick against Denis and magically a bunch of flowers appears*)
Denis Cor. Magic, Granny!
Granny Of course. Now Denis, help me unload the grot stock.
Denis The grot stock.
Granny Whilst I unlock the burglar-proof shop door. Silence please.

The lights dim

Denis Quiet everyone.

Granny makes a magic gesture in the air, a very funny sequence of movements, then finally points at the door. A magic chord is heard and the door flies open

Granny Heave ho, Denis, in we go.
Denis Right Granny. Now I'll unload all the grot stock.

They go into Granny's shop

Granny While I unlock the grot stock box. (*Pointing to a large chest, rather like a treasure chest*) Silence please.

The lights dim again while Granny goes through the same dotty ritual, then, as she points a finger, we hear the magic chord and the lid of the chest flies open

Denis Blimey. She's done it again!

Granny starts to sort out the contents of the wheelbarrow

Granny Right, Denis. Here we go. One used can of paint. Nice colour. (*She passes it to Denis*)
Denis One can of used paint. Nice colour. (*He puts it in the chest*)
Granny (*picking up a saucepan*) One tin helmet.
Denis One tin helmet. (*He tries it on before bunging it in the chest*)
Granny One jar, empty.
Denis One jar ... (*he starts to undo the lid*) ... empty ...(*A trick snake flies out as he removes the lid*) Gor blimey. That frightened me to death. Me dustbin gloves 'ave gorn all wobbly. Look at that. (*He shows the audience that he's got the shakes*)
Granny Never mind, Denis. It'll do for the budgie's tea. Now, one useful hammer. (*She passes him a big trick hammer with a rubber head*)
Denis One useful hammer.

Denis bangs his head with it. We hear a "motor horn" sound as it makes contact. He goes temporarily squiffy)

Granny ... and a collection of the (*throws a magazine*) ...

Denis catches as she throws

... most (*throws*) interesting (*throws*) magazines (*throws*) that (*throws*) I (*throws*) have (*throws*) ever (*throws*) seen!

Granny throws the last one—this sequence should be practised until it can be accomplished with great speed and skill

Denis Time for a sit down, then.
Granny Quite. I know what should perk me up.
Denis What's that, Granny?
Granny A slug of the old "Grot Tonic". (*She extracts, a bottle from her knicker leg, swigs, makes funny noises and passes it to Denis*) How 'bout you, Denis?

Denis is about to take it

Or would you prefer some of my turnip tea?
Denis Turnip tea? Great!
Granny Good choice, Denis, my old dustbin. Do you know that this is brewed (*pouring a mug of tea from a huge demi-john*) from one of Great Grandma Grot's recipes?
Denis Should be good then.

Granny brings the mug to Denis

Granny Yes, indeed.

Granny keeps holding out the mug to Denis during the dialogue and just as he goes to take it, she absent-mindedly takes it out of his reach

Do you know, Denis, you wouldn't believe the things I've brought back from the tip today. The most splendiferous grot. People do throw away the most extraordinary things you know.

Act I

Denis Well, (*getting the mug at last*) it's funny you should say that Granny. Cos we've been 'avin' a rummage around in old Slickerbotham's bin and we've found some real brill stuff for you. Haven't we kids?
Granny Really?
Denis Yup. Now, close your eyes, Granny.

Granny closes her eyes

No peeping.
Granny This is gorgeous. I love surprises, just like Christmas.

Denis leads Granny outside to see the rubbish collected by the children

Denis Here we are. Right. Now you can open your eyes.
Granny (*amazed and delighted*) I'm absolutely flabbergrotted, Denis. My grotty has never been so flabbered. This is superb. What have we got?

Denis hands her the inflated "whoopee" cushion—she presses it

Lovely, that can be my new front doorbell. (*She puts it in the wheelbarrow*)

Denis hands her Freda's knickers

One strainer for my hiccup potion. (*She puts them in the wheelbarrow*)

Denis hands her the broken umbrella

A useful basket or an umbrella for when the sun's shining (*She puts it in the wheelbarrow*)
Denis (*pulling out a couple of saveloys*) And a couple of ear plugs, (*he puts them on either ear*) for when Harold's playing his "Heavy Metal" records. (*He hands one to Granny*)
Granny (*munching the sausage*) Excellent, Denis. Well, you've all done very well indeed. Congrotulations! Dear, dear. Poor Mr Slickerbotham—he really has so little imagination. Fancy throwing such useful things away.
Denis Horrendous. (*He chucks the sausage into the audience*)
Granny Ungrotful! (*She chucks the sausage into the audience*) Well, Denis, I must really make a move and begin the day's work. Much to be done. (*She lifts up her skirt and removes from her knicker leg a long roll of paper, like a till receipt*) Just hold on to this end please, Denis, there's a dear chap.

As she checks her list, she unrolls it and, unaware of the fact, winds it round Denis's body

Now where did I put my glasses? (*She pats herself all over—the audience point out that they are round her neck*) Can you spot them? Oh, of course, round my neck. What a silly Grotty I am to be sure. Now! (*She puts on her glasses and goes through the list*) This is my list! On it are all the things I have to do today, because you see I'm very forgetful at times. Now. What do I have to get done? One—sort out seven woolly socks for Mrs Thompson's strange children. Two—a pair of mini-plimsolls for Professor Patterson's parrot, Percy. Three—prepare one large box of assorted grot for Woolworths, the clothing department, and Four (*she titters*) two packets of special . . . . (*She giggles*)

Denis giggles

. . . stinkbombs (*hysterical*) for the Vicar!

They fall about holding stomachs

Denis (*recovering*) Blimey, you've got a week's work there, Granny.
Granny Indeed I have, Denis. So let's get cracking. Denis, can you give me a hand?

Denis busts out of the till roll, collects it up and puts it into the wheelbarrow

Denis I expect I can stay for about 'arf an 'our. Charlie's still down the factory, I expect. Chattin' up Pickle Lily. (*To the audience*) Get it? Picallili. (*He laughs — they don't*)
Granny Oh, glory be, Denis. What awful jokes. Mind you — you certainly know your onions! (*She roars with laughter — nobody else does*) Oh well, never mind. Come along. Sorting out to be done.
Denis 'Ere 'ang on, Granny, we ain't gonna get through this lot on our tod.
Granny Mmmm. You could be right, Denis. There's an awful lot to do.
Denis Well, how about asking all our mates here to give us a hand?
Granny (*to the audience*) Would you? Would you help me to sort out these jobs? I say, I would be most grotified if you could. Wonderful!

They go into the shop for various boxes to hand out to parts of the audience

Now, Denis, the socks should lie in that box there.

Denis opens the box and pulls out an old kipper

Denis This can't be right, Granny.
Granny Grotious me no — that's last week's supper. They must be in here. (*She indicates another box*) Now, Denis, you get your lot to sort out the socks and Woolworth's grot — while I deal with Parrot Paraphernalia and Pong, Poos and Perfumes!

They hand out the boxes to separate groups in the audience, giving instructions as to what they require sorting out. There is a great hullabaloo and kerfuffle, rushing from one group to the other. They shout things like: "Got the plimsolls? Fantastic! Eventually, all is sorted out and Granny and Denis carry the highly coloured boxes back to the shop, thanking the audience profusely. A great deal of "ad lib" comedy from the two characters

Well, all done. In record time.
Denis I should say so. Thanks very much everyone.
Granny Yes, indeed. Thank you! Now, I must get the labels for addressing. (*She goes to potter around the shelves*)

Meanwhile Denis is clearing away debris

Denis Granny? What do you reckon to Old Slickerbotham and his two spooky assistants over there?

Act I

Granny 'Er, beg pardon, Denis?
Denis Slickerbotham. What d'ye think of 'im?
Granny Oh... old Slobberchops... yes, well. (*She moves to Denis. In a low whisper*) I don't like him, Denis, to be quite honest, he's not quite right somehow.
Denis What d'ye mean—not quite right?
Granny Funny.
Denis Loony?
Granny No, not loony. Just odd somehow.
Denis You can say that again...
Granny Just odd, somehow.

During the next sequence of dialogue, they bend their knees, getting lower and lower. The dialogue is fast

Denis No! I mean I agree with you. Look, he's been there two months now right?
Granny Right.
Denis It's supposed to be a dry cleaners, right?
Granny Right.
Denis And yet over the period of two months, we've not seen any stuff being delivered. That's wrong.
Granny Right.
Denis An even more mysterious we 'aven't seen...
Granny No customers.
Denis Right. So what they doin' in there, 'oovering and cleanin' morning, noon and night?

They both shoot upright

Granny I don't know, Denis. But I'll tell you something. (*Using her binoculars*) I wouldn't mind having a quick butcher's hook inside.
Denis (*excited*) You mean burglarize the place?
Granny Certainly not, Denis. I mean we could (*she winks at the audience and falls into Denis' arms*) accidentally fall through the front door.
Denis But 'ow we gonna do that? Old Slicker B always keeps that door locked. He's most particular about that.
Granny Yes, well, what we need to do, dear, is "borrow" the key.
Denis But 'ow, Granny?
Granny Yes—how?

They look at each other

Suddenly there are loud crashes, bangs, shrieks from Slickerbotham in his shop. We can hear Edith howling and Harold laughing

Slickerbotham GET THAT CHILD OUT OF HERE!!!

Clarissa and Freda enter, pushing, with great force, the pram containing Harold. Clarissa is holding a milk jug and Freda a sugar basin

Denis rushes forward and saves Harold and the pram. A huge can of Guinness is ejected from the pram, which Granny catches and finishes

Clariss and Freda go back into the shop and throw out Edith's coat and bag

Edith, Clarissa, Freda and Slickerbotham, holding a pair of tongs from which is suspended a dripping nappy, enter

Edith (*tearfully*) Please, Mr Slickerbotham. It won't happen again. Harold don't mean any harm. It was just an 'orrible mistake.
Slickerbotham Mistake!
Freda Miscalculation.
Clarissa Data Error.
Freda Fault.
Clarissa Data Error.
Freda Fault.
Slickerbotham Terminate.
Clarissa ⎫
Freda ⎬ (*together*) Beep! (*They freeze*)
Slickerbotham (*brandishing the nappy*) Dropping his nappy in the teapot—a mistake? (*He hands the nappy to Freda. Pointing to the milk jug*) Dribbling in the milk jug—a mistake? (*Taking the sugar bowl and sticking it under Edith's nose*) PIDDLING IN THE SUGAR!!! You call that a MISTAKE!
Harold Ha! Ha!
Slickerbotham That brat is the mistake. It is ill-mannered and worse, it is unhygienic?
Harold Wotchit, mate!
Freda Filthy!
Clarissa Disgusting!
Freda Germy!
Clarissa Disgusting!
Slickerbotham Terminate.

Clarissa and Freda "beep"

(*To Edith*) And your employment is, as of this very moment, terminated.
Edith (*disbelieving*) When?
Slickerbotham Now!
Freda Immediately!
Clarissa Forthwith!
Freda Toute suite!
Clarissa Straight away!
Freda Toute suite!
Clarissa Straight away!
Slickerbotham (*to Freda and Clarissa*) Oh, shut up!

Freda and Clarissa "beep"

Sad melodramatic "Hearts and Flowers" music plays

Edith Oh no! Please, Mr Slickerbotham. I need the money. (*Tearfully*) How will Harold and I manage with Archie gorn and everything?

Harold is crying and the rest follow

Act I   13

If you tried Mr Slickerbotham, you could grow to love Harold like me.

Music fades

Harold Daddy. (*He makes kissing noises*)
Granny And me. (*She wipes away her tears*)
Denis And me. (*He wipes his nose*) He's a lovely little lad.
Harold Lovely.
Denis When you get to know him.
Slickerbotham (*sneering*) Lovely?
Freda Little?
Clarissa Lad?
Slickerbotham More like nasty!

Harold growls

Freda Smelly!
Clarissa Thing!

Harold emits a loud burp

Freda ⎫
Clarissa ⎭ (*together*) EEeaaaarghhh!
Edith There, now you've upset Harold. Poor little lamb.
Harold Baaa!
Edith (*clouting the pram*) Don't be stupid, Harold.
Granny Mr Saggy Bags, you can't give this charming young lady the sack.
Denis Not just chuck her out on to the street.
Slickerbotham Yes. Out on to the street, into the gutter, where she and that creature both belong. Come Clarissa.
Clarissa Beep!
Slickerbotham Freda.
Freda Beep!
Slickerbotham Let us go.
Clarissa Depart.
Freda Toodle-oo.
Clarissa Depart.
Freda Toodle-oo.
Slickerbotham Terminate.

Clarissa and Freda both "beep"
Slickerbotham, Clarissa and Freda turn as one and start to depart as Harold's spotty faces emerges from the pram

Harold Bum faces!

They freeze, horrified. Granny is taken aback, Edith and Denis snigger

Freda ⎫
Slickerbotham ⎬ (*together*) What!
Clarissa ⎭
Harold You need a clean-up! (*He fires a water pistol at them and liberally all over the audience*)

Slickerbotham, Freda and Clarissa scream and run back into the shop

Edith (*picking up her coat and bag*) Oh, Harold, what shall we do now?
Harold Have a drinkie! (*He shoots back into his pram*)
Granny (*clapping her hands*) Quite right, Harold. Drinkies for us all. Turnip teas all round, eh Denis?
Harold Turnip teas—muck? I wanna a Guiness. (*He bangs the inside of his pram*)
Granny Well, I don't know about that, Harold.
Edith Guinness is good for you.
Denis He's a growing lad.
Harold Big boy.
Edith (*whispering*) Don't upset him anymore, please. I had a terrible do this morning over his electric razor.

The sound of an electric razor is heard coming from the pram. Granny exchanges glances with Denis

Granny All right, my dear. Of course. Don't worry. We've all had a very nasty experience. I suggest we all retire to the back parlour for a mug of turnip tea, a SMALL Guinness.
Harold Yipee!
Granny And you must tell us all you know about Slickerbags and those two strange assistants of his.
Denis Yeah. We was just talking about how peculiar that dry cleaning place of his, is.
Edith But what about my job, Miss Grot?
Granny Don't worry about the job, my dear. I can do with some extra help in the shop. And please do not address me as Miss Grot. My name is Granny. And I should like both you and Harold to think of me as your Granny.
Harold Granny.
Edith Oh. How ever can I thank you. Granny Grot? Did you hear, Harold, my little cherub? Granny's gonna help us.

Harold blows a raspberry

Granny (*uncertainly*) Y—e—e—s.

The Lights fade slowly on Granny Grot's shop as she ushers them into the back parlour and out of view—as lights come up at SLICKERBOTHAM's shop. The lights are cold and blue

  Slickerbotham enters in a fury followed by Freda and Clarissa

Slickerbotham Gone? What do you mean, gone?
Freda Disappeared.
Clarissa Vanished.
Freda Escaped.
Clarissa Gorn off!
Slickerbotham Terminate!

Clarissa and Freda both "beep"

Act I

When? And how? You—you hopeless hooverettes.
Freda Today. Door left open.
Clarissa Tea lady sacked. No one on duty.
Freda Germ must be loose in the street.
Clarissa I can smell it. Close at hand. (*She sniffs around*)
Slickerbotham Then find it, you foolish floorcloths. It is essential to the successful outcome of our "cleansing campaign".
Freda Purifying plans.
Clarissa Dirt destruction.
Slickerbotham Exactly. If we can successfully purify the Megagerm . . .
Clarissa ⎫
Freda ⎭ (*together*) The Megagerm. Ughh!!
Slickerbotham . . . a monstrous conglomeration of all the filthier habits that children possess like . . .
Freda Sticky fingers.
Clarissa Dirty lug 'oles.
Freda Grotty nostrils.
All Ugh! eeaarrch! eeEEAARRRCCCCHHHH!!!

Slickerbotham grabs a chair and speaks like a dictator as Freda and Clarissa kneel in awe and obeissance

Slickerbotham *If* we can purify the germ, then we will be certain that we have total power. The ultimate power to ensure that every child everywhere will be spotless and deodorized. Then—after the children—the grown-ups. All those parents who fail to punish their children for getting into these filthy states. We will punish them for their disgusting depravities. Then you will see the world as it could be. As it will be. As I SHALL MAKE IT!!!
Freda No more sandcastles.
Clarissa No football in the mud.
Freda Out with tomato sauce.
Clarissa Down with jam doughnuts.
Freda Forbid ice-cream.
Clarissa Destroy CHIPS!!
Slickerbotham (*cackling*) Good. Very good. Excellent. In my new sterile world every family will be provided with State . . .
Freda Scum scrapers.
Clarissa Fungus freezers.
Freda Grime gungers.
Slickerbotham . . . and?
All (*sotto voce*) Bogey Blasters!

They break into inane cackles

Slickerbotham All children to receive three baths a day. Morning . . .

Freda and Clarissa rub their faces

. . . noon . . .

Freda and Clarissa rub their armpits

... and night ...

Freda and Clarissa rub their bottoms

Hair to be inspected and combed at all schools and places of employment on the hour.

Freda \
Clarissa / (*together*) Every hour!

Freda Nit nurses in attendance at cinemas and discos.

Slickerbotham Stronger soap.

Freda Stiffer starch.

Clarissa Bigger bogs!

All (*quietly*) Grime is a crime. (*Louder*) Grime is a crime. (*Very loud*) Grime is a crime!

During this, Megagerm, who is lurking at one of the stage entrances, starts to make revolting, unrefined, unpurified noises and wallows on to the area. It is a large, formless amoebic shape, black and green, covered in weals, fungus, pustules, boils and general nasty things. It is an actor in a bag, who rolls and winds and wriggles. It gets among the kids and causes havoc, crawling over adults and squeezing little ones

Freda \
Clarissa / (*together*) The Megagerm! Help!

Slickerbotham There it is! The noxious creature. Quickly, protective clothing.

Freda The net.

Clarissa Sterilizing sprays.

Slickerbotham, Freda and Clarissa exit

Megagerm tries to climb over the audience. It is funny and outrageous rather than frightening

Slickerbotham, Freda and Clarissa enter bringing with them the "Processor"—a huge machine with two doors and covered in advertisements for detergents etc. Freda carries a large net and Clarissa carries a large spray labelled "Super Sterilizer". There is an ad lib chase. They capture Megagerm and take him towards the "Processor"

Clarissa \
Freda / (*together*) We will purify this revolting heap.

Slickerbotham Into the machine without delay! Now. ... Turn on the Processor to Level eight.

Freda Level eight.

Clarissa Confirmed.

The machine starts to make pseudo-scientific disintegrating noises

Slickerbotham (*emotionally*) It is a far far better thing that I do now than I have ever done.

Freda *Tale of Two Cities.*

Clarissa Chapter Fifteen.

Act I   17

Slickerbotham Shut up!

Megagerm, who has been struggling and protesting in amoebic language, is pushed into the door marked "BEFORE". The door snaps shut and there is a tremendously loud rattling and banging, processing shrieks and grindings, strobe lights, smoke. We can see brushes and brooms beating and cleaning

Slickerbotham Five seconds to final rinse.

Freda and Clarissa turn down the Processor dial, as they count, to zero

Freda Five.
Clarissa Four.
Freda Three.
Clarissa Two.
Slickerbotham ONE! Open!

Freda opens the door marked "AFTER". Megagerm emerges in a white bag. He emits small, clean, pure whimpers

Slickerbotham Success!

Freda and Clarissa applaud

Now we see a purified Megagerm!
Freda Triumph!
Clarissa Victory!
Slickerbotham Remove it and place it in container X four five one and then return here immediately. (*Addressing the audience*) See what happens to foolish filth. Beware all those that have dirty fingernails, you cannot escape us. You cannot hide. We will track you down in the dark and then (*pause*) the NET!! (*He cackles insanely*) Silence, there is too much jollity. The final stage of the Master Plan must now be executed.
Freda Completed.
Clarissa Finished 'orf.
Slickerbotham (*striding into the centre of the street*) Who is the most vile blot on this landscape? What spotty smudge or smear makes our lives unbearable? Can you name this ultimate in FILTH!
Freda \
Clarissa / (*together*) Yes, master.
Slickerbotham Then speak his unspeakable name!
Freda \
Clarissa / (*together*) Horrible Harold!
Slickerbotham Exactly. The Processor has proved successful and all powerful on the Megagerm. Now let us put it to the hardest of all possible human tests. For surely there is no living creature more repellent than the repulsive child.
Freda When shall we persuade him to step into the Processor, master.
Slickerbotham Persuade him? We shall *snatch* him *tonight*. Come, there are more important plans to be made. We must take him to our pre-processing laboratory in the old empty house by Mason's Yard. Once there—perfect my plans, purify my panties and perchance to dream!

Freda
Clarissa } (*together*) Aye, there's the rub!

They exit into the shop, cackling

The sounds of the Processor are heard as the house lights slowly come up to full

CURTAIN

ACT II

It is evening. The street lamps are dimly lit. We hear a dog bark from a long way off and a cat meow close-by

Edith enters singing and pushing Harold to the front of the shop for his evening sleep, unless Harold has been left out during the Interval for the audience to look at and talk to

Edith (*singing*) Rock-a-bye Harold in this big pram
Rock-a-bye Harold, my little lamb
When Dad comes 'ome
We'll have such a ball
Out will come Harold, Guinness and all.
Harold (*sadly*) Daddy ...
Edith (*fussing around his clothing*) There we are, my little tinker. Who's Mummy's precious then? Eh? Coochy, coochy, coo.
Harold (*sniffing*) I want my Daddy. (*He gives a big sniff*)
Edith I know. I know, my darlin'. I know how much you miss your Dad. So do I lovey. (*She sniffs*)
Harold Write a letter!
Edith Letter? Oh yes, that is a good idea, Harold. We could send a letter to the M.L.D.
Harold Wozzat?
Edith M.L.D.? Ministry for Lost Dads, Harold. They're specialists.
Harold Goody. Goody.
Edith I've already contacted the most important people, Harold. British Rail Lost Property Office, Battersea Dog's Home, Brick Street Sewage Disposal Company ... but a personal letter to the Minister—that should get everyone in the country keeping an eye open for my Archie.
Harold (*thrusting paper and pencil out*) Write it, Mummy!
Edith Clever lad! (*Taking the paper and pencil she begins to write*) Now. Let me see—yes—Dear Minister, Lost, one Dad.
Harold My Dad.
Edith Last seen grasping ham sandwich belonging to son, Harold.
Harold That's me.
Edith Please find, return as soon as possible—with best wishes.
Harold Best wishes ...
Edith Er, how can I finish it, Harold?
Harold "Harold's Mummy".
Edith 'Course that's perfect. I'll get Denis to pop it in the letter-box. It should catch the last post.
Harold Put up some posters!

Edith Oh yes—we must get him to put up a couple of posters, too. Don't you worry, darlin', your Dad'll turn up somewhere. 'E's never let us down before. (*Calling*) Denis! (*She puts the letter in an envelope, and proffers it to Harold*) Lickies.

Harold licks it and then Edith addresses it

There's a good boy.

Denis enters carrying a baby's bottle, a spider, cigarettes and a huge polystyrene sandwich

Denis I've brought Harold's night-time bottle and 'is toys. (*He hands over the bottle containing Guinness, the spider, the packet of cigarettes and the huge sandwich*)
Edith Thanks, Den. Could you pop this in the post-box and ...
Harold (*holding up the posters*) Posters, Mummy!
Edith Oh yes, and put a couple of posters up?
Denis Yes, of course I will Edie. Night, night, Harold. Sleep well. See you in the morning.
Harold Night, night, Denis.

Denis puts up the posters then exits

Edith (*handing the items to Harold*) Here's your bottle.
Harold Guinness, hooray!
Edith Twenty Benson and Hedges, luxury length, only the best for my boy. (*Giving him the spider*) Here's your Wally.
Harold It's Wally! It's Wally!
Edith And a little something in case you feel peckish in the night. (*She gives him the sandwich*)
Harold (*making horrible gormandizing noises*) Can't eat it all. (*He throws out bits of the sandwich*)
Edith Oh, you were hungry, Harold. All happy now?
Harold (*jumping for joy and bashing Wally*) Take that, Wally. I'll smash yer face in.
Edith Now stop fighting with Wally, there's a good boy and settle down nicely.

Denis enters

Denis OK. All done.
Edith Ssh!
Denis (*quickly*) Oh yeah, well time for a bit of shut-eye. Granny's aired all the spare beds.
Edith (*whispering*) Night, Harold.
Harold Night, night.
   (*Singing*)   Rock-a-bye Wally,
                  'Ere comes a thump!

A tremendous battle ensues and all hell is let loose in the pram

Act II

Edith
Denis } (*together*) Harold!!

There is silence

> *Edith and Denis exit on tiptoe turning down a sign saying "Danger Do Not Disturb" on the side of the pram*
>
> *The lights fade and as they go down the sound of a match being struck comes from the pram and a glow appears as Harold lights a cigarette. After a moment "spooky" music is played and a ghostly blue light comes up on the Dry Cleaning Emporium*
>
> *Slickerbotham jumps out followed by Freda who is carrying a net and then Clarissa with a Stun Spray*

Slickerbotham (*leaping in*) Ah ha! The "snatching hour" is nigh.

They point towards the sleeping Harold on each of their words

Freda (*leaping in*) Snatch!
Clarissa (*leaping in*) Catch!
All Trap!!
Slickerbotham Is the net prepared?
Freda Net. (*She twirls it menacingly but accidently entangles Slickerbotham*)
Slickerbotham Stupid twit. Anaesthetic Spray?
Clarissa Primed. (*She accidentally sprays Slickerbotham*)
Slickerbotham Fool! Quickly, the song.

They advance towards Harold's pram and sing as they go

All   Rock-a-bye Harold, here comes the spray
              Soon you'll be bye byes and far far away
              You'll be Oh-so spotless
              You'll be Oh-so clean
              When we've passed you through
              Our process machine. (*They cackle*)

Slickerbotham Now, you remember the plan? Stun spray first, then the "net". There must be no mistakes.
Freda Errors.
Clarissa Faults. (*She drops the spray*)

Freda and Slickerbotham give Clarissa suffering looks

Slickerbotham This spotty creature is a slippery customer and not as big a fool as he makes out.
Freda Crafty.
Clarissa Deviously underhand.

Freda and Slickerbotham do a double take

Slickerbotham Once he is unconscious and in our power, we must take him firstly to the pre-processing experimental laboratory in Mason's Yard. For what my friends?

Freda Tests.
Clarissa Anatomical and analytical procedures. (*She is getting too big for her boots*)
Slickerbotham ⎫
Freda ⎭ (*together*) Shut up! (*They clout Clarissa*)

Harold sings, a lullaby to Wally. They freeze until noise subsides

Slickerbotham Advance with stealth. At least the creature is dozing and unarmed.
Harold That's what you think!

Harold sprays Slickerbotham, Clarissa and Freda with a plastic streamer can. They all shriek "dirt", "filth", "contamination", etc.

Slickerbotham Quick, the spray, pathetic purifiers!

They spray the pram and throw the net over it, ad-lib havoc. Harold's face appears for a moment, he is sprayed and zonks out

Insensible.
Freda Zapped.
Clarissa Zonked.

Slickerbotham, Freda and Clarissa cackle

Slickerbotham Quickly, help me lift this contaminated contraption into the street. Speed is essential.
Freda Vital.
Clarissa Imperative.

Freda and Clarissa lift the pram and find it heavy

Slickerbotham Monstrous burden.
Freda Vast bulk.
Clarissa (*with feeling*) Bleedin' heavy.

Slickerbotham runs up to zebra crossing and looks both ways

Slickerbotham The coast is clear. Come. To the laboratory.

They are about to cross the zebra crossing when they all freeze

All EEK!
Slickerbotham What is it?
Freda ⎫
Clarissa ⎭ (*together*) Earwigs!

They watch as the "earwigs" progress across the crossing, to the accompaniment of "earwig" music

Slickerbotham (*when they have crossed*) Away!
Freda Depart!
Clarissa Earwigs go!
Slickerbotham Shut up!

Act II   23

Harold Help! Help! I've been snatched! I want my Mum! I don't want to be experimented on!

Slickerbotham, Clarissa and Freda exit with Harold, cackling noisily

Granny Grot and Denis enter, wakened by the noise. Granny wears a long Victorian nightie and mob-cap. Denis wears a dressing-gown and his dustman's cap. Granny carries a medieval mace

Edith enters walking backwards, she is wearing a bright orange baby-doll nightie, an orange plastic cap over a hair net and curlers and a white face-pack

Denis Blimey, what on earth was that racket?
Granny What's up, Denis? Not burglars, I hope?
Denis Dunno. I just heard strange sounds and ...

Edith bumps into Denis and Granny and as she turns they see the white face-pack and shriek

Denis
Granny } *(together)* Eek! (*Denis jumps into Granny's arms*)
Edith What's up?
Granny Nothing to concern yourself with, my dear—we just thought we heard ...
Edith Aaaiieeeooouuuuu!!! (*Pointing to the empty spot where the pram stood*) Where's my little lambkin?
Denis Blimey, he's been snatched!
Granny Completely disappeared, just like his unfortunate father.
Edith Oh, my gawd. 'Arold! 'Arold! (*She calls and runs up and down the street*)

Denis and Granny also run up and down the street

Edith turns to the audience and finds out, ad lib, a. What happened to Harold? b. Who's taken him? c. Where have they taken him to?

Denis (*stopping the discussion with a whistle*) What you found out then?
Granny Well, that ghastly Mr Slickerbotham and his creepy assistants have kidnicked Harold.
Denis Taken him 'orf to some kind of experimental place.
Edith Experimental? I'm not havin' strange people muckin' about with my Harold. We must do something.
Granny An' quick.
Denis Right.
Granny Now, Denis. First things first. You know this area well. Any ideas as to where Slickerbotham might have this horrendous hide-out?
Edith Think, Denis.

Denis paces up and down

He's thinking.

Denis Well, it's only a hunch, mind, but I've seen him disappear into a dark basement place down the back of Mason's Yard. It's not far from here.
Edith I do hope you're right, Denis. (*Addressing the audience*) It's Harold's chest I worry about, with the cold and everything. And will he have enough to eat and drink. He goes bananas when he's deprived.
Granny Don't worry Edith. I have complete faith in Denis. Now, suppose while Edith and I take this opportunity to have a closer dekko at the inside of that (*pointing*) so-called dry cleaning establishment, you make your way down to Mason's Yard as quickly as possible.
Denis You're on, Granny. You nip in and get changed. I'll see you back here in about ten minutes.

Denis takes off his dressing-gown and hands it to Granny

Granny Excellent. C'mon Edith. Work to be done.
Edith Do be careful Denis and do try to bring Harold back safely.
Denis Don't you fret yourself, Edith, see you soon.
Edith All right, Denis.

Denis exits

But it's such a worry. Poor Harold. What's going to happen to my little lambkin?
Granny C'mon Edith, old girl. Snap out of it. Follow me.

Edith and Granny exit

The lights fade to a black-out. Sinister music is heard. During the black-out, Slickerbotham, Freda and Clarissa bring on a white laboratory table. On it are white surgical gloves, syringes, a microscope, test-tubes with multi-coloured liquids, retorts etc. The lights come up slowly

Denis enters—creeping

Denis Blimey, what a spookiferous place. This must be old Slickerbotham's experimental lab. Where he does experiments and that. I must have beaten 'em 'ere by taking the short cut. Good. That will give me time to 'ave a look around.
Slickerbotham (*off*) This way, bring the pram down the cellar steps.

Harold cries "Ouch" offstage as they bump down each step

Hurry, hurry.

Loud bumping noises off

Denis Watch out. They're comin'. Quick, help me hide.

Slickerbotham, Clarissa and Freda enter wheeling Harold

A bright green light comes up on the table

Slickerbotham This way. Quickly.
Denis (*whispering*) Blimey, they've got young Harold.
Slickerbotham Now, scientific sisters, before we return to the shop and place this—this monstrous lump ...

Act II

Harold Don't be rude!
Denis Cor, that's a bit strong, init?
Slickerbotham ... into the Processor and thereby enable the machine to face its final challenge, we must ensure that there are no physical complications. (*Slickerbotham picks up an axe and feels the edge*
Harold Blimey—he's gonna chop bits off me.
Freda Problems.
Clarissa Difficulties.
Slickerbotham Just so. (*Picking up a saw*) We must carry out routine tests on the infected infant

Clariss and Freda make sawing noises

Are you ready?
Denis They'd better not 'urt Harold.
Freda Ready.
Clarissa Willing.
Freda \
Clarissa / (*together*) And able.
Slickerbotham Right. One. Listen to heart and pulse rate.
Freda \
Clarissa / (*together*) Listen to heart and pulse rate.

Freda puts on the stethoscope and plunges the end into the pram. Out of the pram comes the deafening roar of a "Heavy Metal" concert. The noise is very short and loud. They all leap back, screaming, holding ears

Denis (*chuckling*) Good old Harold.
Slickerbotham Astounding.
Freda Amazing.
Clarissa Abnormal!
Slickerbotham Second test. Lung capacity of the bronchial brat.
Freda \
Clarissa / (*together*) Lung capacity of the bronchial brat.
Freda (*taking a huge pin*) Surgical probe entry.
Clarissa Now!

Harold lets out terrific scream/roar which blows down Slickerbotham and his assistants

Harold Blimey, that went right up Wally's nose. (*He holds up Wally*)
Slickerbotham Noisy.
Freda Nasty.
Clarissa Normal.
Slickerbotham Test number three. The brain scan.
Freda \
Clarissa / (*together*) The brain scan.
Denis Crikey. They're only going to look inside Harold's bonce!
Freda Removing brain now!
Harold Ouch!

Freda produces a small green pea—they all cackle

Slickerbotham Pathetic.
Freda Puerile.
Clarissa (*looking at it through binoculars*) Pea-brain!
Slickerbotham Test four. Sample of blood from the lymphatic lout!
Freda ⎫
Clarissa ⎭ (*together*) Sample of blood from the lymphatic lout!
Denis I hope Harold can take all this.
Harold Not more needles!
Freda Syringe ready.
Clarissa Now!

Freda plunges the syringe into the pram. The syringe is substituted by Harold for one that is full of Guinness

The sample is placed in a flask

Harold Ow! That went right in my botty!
Slickerbotham Excellent. Now. Slide. (*He walks to the microscope*)

Freda and Clarissa do a slide across the floor like a couple of kids in the snow

Freda ⎫
Clarissa ⎭ (*together*) Wheee!
Slickerbotham No, stupid imbeciles! Microscopic slides.
Freda ⎫
Clarissa ⎭ (*together, realizing their error*) Oh!

Freda and Clarissa do the same slide except it is a very small movement now

Slickerbotham (*beside himself with anger*) Brainless buffoons! Slide-for-the-microscope!
Freda Misunderstanding.
Clarissa Cock-up.
Freda Slide prepared.

A slide is prepared and placed under the microscope and as Slickerbotham peers into eye piece, the Lights dim accompanied by a tremulous, single chord. When the Lights come up Slickerbotham stands open-mouthed, completely flabbergasted by what he has seen

Slickerbotham Impossible! My eyes must be deceiving me. In all my years fighting filth and muck I have never seen anything like this.
Freda ⎫
Clarissa ⎬ (*together*) What is it? What is it?
Denis ⎪
Harold ⎭
Slickerbotham The main ingredient of this blood appears to be undiluted . . .
Freda ⎫
Clarissa ⎬ (*together*) Yes? Yes?
Harold ⎪
Denis ⎭

Act II

Slickerbotham Guinness!!!
Harold Yahoo! (*He burps*)
Denis Good old Harold.
Slickerbotham Enough. The tests are concluded. There is no doubt in my mind that this ulcerous article is perfect material for the Processor. Let us return to the place of purification as quickly as possible.

They start to remove objects as the Lights fade

Harold No! Not the Process machine! Wally can't swim! Help!

Slickerbotham, Freda, Clarissa and Harold exit

Denis (*watching them disappear*) Blimey! No time to waste. I must get back and warn the others.

Denis exits

The Lights fade to dimly light Granny Grot's shop

Granny Grot and Edith enter through the auditorium, flashing their torches. Granny has a large black cloak on and Edith is wearing her mac

Granny (*whispering*) Ready Edith. On tiptoe. Remember we mustn't make a sound in the street.
Edith Oh, Granny. It's such a worry bein' a mum.
Granny Quite, but remember that Mum's the word. (*She puts a finger to her lips*)
Edith OK.

They walk stealthily up the street in unison, each step is registered by the sound of a Glockenspiel—when they reach the shop, they stop and look around, illuminating the area with their torches

Granny Not a sign of a soul. That's excellent!
Edith That's super, Granny, but the only thing that worries me—is how are we are going to get in?
Granny No problem to Granny Grot. "Art" is one of my specialities. One of my many talents. Watch carefully, Edith, and you will see the maxim "the pen is mightier than the sword" proved true. (*She extricates a large felt-tip pen from her cloak and proceeds to draw a keyhold on the shop door*)
Edith What are you doing, Granny?
Granny Patience, Edith. Patience. This pen can also be the "key" to our problem. (*She pushes the pen into the false keyhole which falls out when pressed, and mimes using the pen as a key turning a lock. The door pushes open*)
Edith (*open-mouthed*) Magic, Granny!
Granny (*rather pleased with herself*) Well, yes. A kind of magic, I suppose. But I like to call it "Breaking and Entering".
Edith (*giggling*) Oh Granny!

Denis creeps in

Denis Pssst.
Edith What's that?
Granny Freeze. Keep absolutely still!
Denis (*still sotto voce*) It's all right, it's only me, Denis.
Granny Oh, Denis. We thought we'd been nabbed.
Denis You *will* be nabbed if you don't hurry up.
Edith Denis, where's Harold?
Denis We were right. Slickerbotham has got 'im.
Edith Oh, no!
Denis Oh, yes! They're headin' back here with 'im—although they seem to be taking a funny route. Anyway, they intend to shove 'im in something they called the "Processor".
Granny Goodness me. Then time is of the essence. Quickly, into the shop.

Lights come up very slowly and dimly light the Dry Cleaning shop

Edith Oooo-er. I ain't been in this part of the shop before.
Denis See if you can spot this Processor thing. (*He accepts any help from the audience*)
Granny Look, here it is. It looks like some kind of machine.
Denis 'Ello. There's a notice or somethin'.
Edith What does it say?
Granny Where are my glasses?
Denis (*putting Granny's glasses on for her*) You've got 'em on, Granny!
Granny Mmmmmm. (*Reading the sign*) Experiment A one nine six completed. Do not touch.
Edith It's like Dr Frankenstein's place.
Granny It's certainly monstrous.
Denis So behind that door must be someone that Slickerbotham's experimented on already?
Granny I'm afraid so, Denis.
Edith Are you gonna 'ave a look?
Denis Yea. Of course. I'm not afraid. Well, not much.
Edith Oh, do be careful, Denis.
Denis Right. Here goes.

Denis opens the door marked "AFTER" to reveal, in the tight spot, a figure wearing white underclothes and clutching a ham sandwich. He is petrified

Edith Oh! My Gawd! It's ARCHIE!!!
Granny Archie?
Denis Harold's Dad.
Granny Of course!
Denis Is he alive?
Granny (*taking out a telescope*) Stand back and let me make a preliminary investigation.

She plonks the big end of the telescope against Archie's chest, and we hear drum beats. It is his heart

Act II   29

Oh, yes. He's alive and raring to go.
Edith But I don't understand. What've they done to him? He's so clean—
   I've never seen him so spotless before.
Denis "Bold Automatic". (*He laughs*)
Granny Actually, you're not far off the mark there, Denis. Automatic might
   be the clue we need to bring Archie back to normality.
Denis You mean "automate" the machine again?
Granny Exactly. With a bit of luck we might be able to "reverse" the
   process and change Archie back to what he was . . . (*She points to the door
   marked "BEFORE"*)
Edith ⎫
Denis ⎭ (*together*) Before!
Granny Bingo! Got it right first time.
Edith 'Ere, he won't come out inside-out and upside-down, will 'e?
Granny Certainly not, Edith. He should be exactly as you remember him.
Denis That's all very nice, Granny, but there's so many knobs and things. I
   mean, which dial do we turn and how far?
Granny Yes . . . (*She turns to the audience and extracts information that the
   central dial turned to level eight does the trick*) This one? To level eight eh?
Denis Let's give it a whirl.
Granny Right, here goes. (*She turns the dial and noises begin inside with lots
   of shrieks and clangs*)
Denis Seems to be working.
Edith I 'ope it's not damaging my Archie. (*To audience*) He's nearly as
   delicate as Harold.
Denis It's stopped.
Granny Stand clear. (*She turns dial back to zero*) I'm going to open it up.
Edith (*seeing herself as an intrepid Girl Guide*) No, Granny. I'm sorry. This
   is one job I must do myself.
Granny Brave girl.

*Edith opens the door and Archie, grubby and smutty emerges. He has a deep
masculine voice*

Archie 'Ere, where am I? And what 'appened to me?
Edith (*cuddling him*) You're safe, Archie and you're home. (*She kisses him
   profusely*) Oh, Archie! (*She hangs on to his arm*)
Granny Good to have you back in Brick Street. (*She shakes Archie's hand*)
Denis How do you feel, Archie?
Archie Well . . . er . . . a bit peckish really. (*He starts to munch the ham
   sandwich*)
Edith That's my Archie!
Archie Here, Edie, where's Harold? Where's the pram?
Granny You might well ask, Archie, old chap. In some danger, I fear.
Denis Slickerbotham's snatched him and intends to use him for an exper-
   iment, just like you.
Edith He's going to stick him in that machine.
Archie Over my ham sandwich! (*He throws the sandwich on the ground*)
Granny That's the stuff. Fighting talk.

They all do a shadow boxing routine

Denis Shh!
Edith What is it, Denis?
Denis I thought I heard something.

We hear Slickerbotham complaining and shouting

Granny You did, Denis. It sounds like Slickerbotham returning with young Harold.
Archie Slickerbotham? I'll "kick his bottom".
Granny Not so hasty, Archie. Let us hide first and observe the situation before deciding on tactics.
Denis Hurry up. Here they come.

They all hide amongst the audience

Freda and Clarissa enter with Slickerbotham who is pushing Harold in the pram. Harold is smoking a cigar and singing "He'll be swimming in the duck pond, when he comes". They are wet and and exhausted and are covered in pond weed

Slickerbotham (*breathlessly*) Don't let that child give any more directions!
Freda Duckpond.
Harold Quack! Quack!
Clarissa Soaking.
Freda Slimey.
Slickerbotham Disgusting! Get the "thing" into the Processor without delay.
Harold No! No!

Freda and Clarissa push the pram towards the Processor

Slickerbotham Fools, look you've left the door of the shop wide open!
Freda Error.
Clarissa Oversight.
Slickerbotham Well, we don't have time to worry about that now. But there'll be no fresh batteries for you at the end of the week. See how you like that.
Freda Miserable.
Clarissa (*slowly*) Run down.
Slickerbotham Yes. Right. (*To Harold*) Imbecilic infant, get out of that ridiculous pram and enter the door. (*He points to the door marked "BEFORE"*) You have laughed your last laugh.
Freda Giggle.
Clarissa Snigger.
Harold Can't!
Slickerbotham What do you mean, you can't?
Harold Dunno what to do!
Slickerbotham Brainless brat! It's simple, you just walk through that door.
Harold What door?
Slickerbotham (*exasperated*) Oohhh! Get him out of that contraption!

Act II

They get Harold out

Freda
Clarissa } *(together, sniggering at Harold's stupidity)* Stupid!

Granny *(popping up and whispering to the others)* By jingo. I think young Harold's got a plan!

Edith If he has—it'll be a good one.

Archie That's my boy!

Denis 'Ere, if he could get Slickerbotham and those two to go inside the door then we could . . .

Granny Do the rest. Stand by!

Slickerbotham Now will you move away from that alcoholic landing craft and push open that door!!!

Harold Don't understand. You'll 'ave to show me.

Slickerbotham Freda. Clarissa.

Freda
Clarissa } *(together)* Master.

Slickerbotham Use the other door *(pointing to the "AFTER" door and instructing them)* and give a "simple" demonstration to this "simple mind".

Freda Nerk!

Clarissa Dumbo!

Freda *(at "AFTER" door)* Open door.

Harold Open door.

Clarissa Enter chamber.

Freda and Clarissa go in

Harold Enter chamber. 'Ere, where they gorn?

Slickerbotham Persil preserve us! In there, you nincompoop! Look, let *me* show you. *(He enters the door)* It's quite simple. You open the door and step inside.

Immediately Harold shuts the door and switches lever to mark eight

Harold Gotcher!!!

Machine starts

Slickerbotham You grotty imbecile! Let me out do you hear?

Granny gets up and charges forward

Granny To the rescue, everyone!

They all join in

Denis Come on, Edith!

Edith Turn the machine up higher!

Archie Give 'em some of their own medicine!

They freeze. Harold stands open-mouthed as he spots Archie

Harold Daddy!!

Archie Chubby chops!

Harold and Archie join hands and do a little dance with Edith

Granny Shall I turn it up higher?
Denis Yeah, I would. I mean, they're ultra-clean and we've got to make them super grotty!
Edith Up to nine then?
Harold Ten!
Granny (*with a mischievous twinkle*) Why not!

When they turn the knob up to ten, the already horrible noises inside are trebled. There is havoc going on inside

Archie Open the door, Denis.

Denis opens the door and out career the three miscreants. They are covered in all kinds of filth and dirt and our "brave band" mock Slickerbotham and the assistants

Edith Stand back, here they come!
Slickerbotham No, aghh! No! Dirt! Filth! I'm contaminated from head to toe! Look! (*He pulls something off his person*)
Freda
Clarissa } (*together*) What?
Slickerbotham A speck of "mucky stuff"!

Freda and Clarissa scream blue murder

Freda Horrible!
Clarissa Horrendous!
Slickerbotham We're as squalid now as all those spotty kids we tried to purify.

They try, frenetically, to wipe off the despoilations from the machine

Stains!
Freda Dandruff! (*She flicks flaked rice from her hair*)
Clarissa (*pulling something from her hair*) Nits! (*She finds a huge bug*)
Slickerbotham Fungus!
Freda Mildew!
Clarissa (*after a pause, quietly horrified*) "Deposits"!
Slickerbotham We must flee the town.
Freda
Clarissa } (*together*) The country.
All The WORLD!!

Slickerbotham, Freda and Clarissa run off with screams and shouts of "horror" spraying the audience with silly string

All HURRAH!!
Edith Good riddance. (*She collects the pram*)
Archie To old rubbish!

Archie puts his arm around Harold

All Hear, hear.

Act II

Granny And now Granny Grot requests the pleasure of your company at her shop for some turnip tea and . . .
Denis Ham sandwiches?

They all laugh

Harold Lovely.
Granny Lovely's the word, Harold. For now we can look forward to some lovely peace around here. The children can play games.
Denis . . . have fun . . .
Harold . . . and git filthy!
Granny Exactly. And I can start collecting some top-notch grot.
Denis I can bang me bins again.
Edith (*sloppily*) I can iron Archie's night-shirt.
Archie And Harold can start school.

Harold freezes in horror

Harold Wot???? School!!! Not likely!! (*He dives back into the pram and resumes his stunted nature*)

Music comes from the pram

Granny Oh, what a pity, Harold , and (*she winks at the others and in a loud deliberate voice says*) I'd heard that the girls at Brick Street Mixed were really something.

The music stops and immediately there is a short pause and we hear Harold say something like "Crumpet" and he dives out again

Edith Just like 'is Dad.
Archie Come on. . . . Let's all go home!

They all exit doing a silly dance, thanking the audience for their help in the adventure. We hear phrases like "pop round and see us any time you like", "anyone want my Motorhead cassettes?". Finally, "The kettle's boiling".

CURTAIN

The Set.

Lamp post.
Raked Seating.
Auditorium Entrance.
Pillar box.
Slicker B's Dust-bin.
Slickerbotham's Dry Cleaners
Street.
Playing Area.
Granny Grot's Shop.
Mrs Thompson's Dustbin
Zebra Crossing.
Lamp post

Slickerbothams.
Sliding door
Auditorium Entrance.
EXIT
Raked Seating.
GRANNY GROTS
Street
The Processor
Zebra Crossing
ramp.
Lamp post
Granny's Dustbin.
Mrs Thompson's Dust-bin.

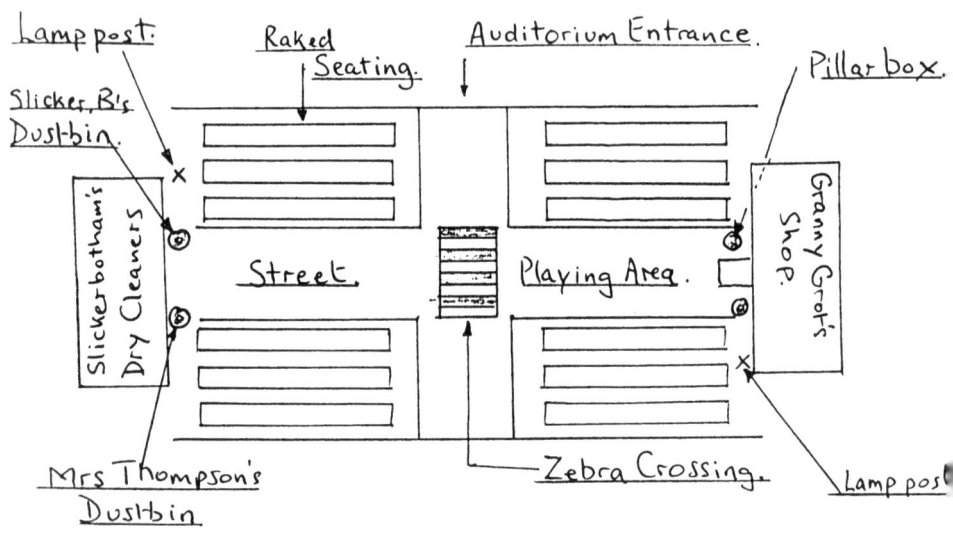

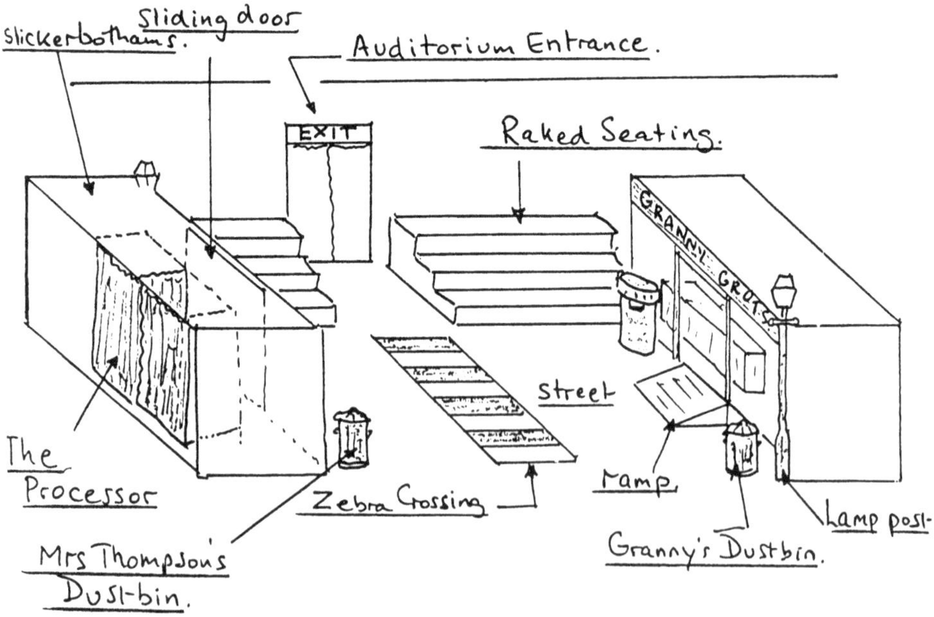

FURNITURE AND PROPERTY LIST

ACT I

On stage: Zebra crossing
Pillar Box
Two lamp posts (optional)
Granny Grot's Shop. *In it:* Assorted grot on shelves, floor, etc., for example:
old books, potion bottles containing coloured water, dressmakers dummy, old telephones. *In shop window:* toothless combs, old toast, used tea-bags, large demi-john labelled "turnip tea", mug, five brightly coloured boxes labelled:
"Grub Grot" containing prop food, old kippers etc.
"Assorted Grot Socks" i.e. lots of odd socks—bright.
"Parrot Paraphernalia" i.e. "Sindy" doll's clothes
"Pongs, Perfumes and Poos"—small bottles, jars, pill-boxes and a box of "stink bombs"
"Assorted Grot"—old and funny clothes
"Grot Stock Box"—a large tin chest with trick wire
Mr Slickerbotham's Shop. *In it:* The "Processor" with two doors marked "Before" and "After"
Three dustbins labelled:
GRANNY GROT'S. *In it:* general rubbish
SLICKERBOTHAM'S. *In it:* two saveloys, a spokeless umbrella, a chamber pot, a bottle labelled "damaged bluebottles" Freda's bloomers, concertina, inflated "whoopee" cushion, string of black sausages
MRS THOMPSON'S. *In it:* newspaper topped with old cabbage and empty cat food tins
A bottle of milk next to Mrs Thompson's dustbin

Off stage: Large pram covered with football slogans, Guinness advertisements and graffiti. *In it:* Cassette player with recordings of (a) Heavy Metal Music (b) "Play School" theme and (c) more Heavy Metal Music. Empty "Monster Munch" packet. Empty Cream Cracker packet. Benson and Hedges Cigarettes. Lighter. Big red sausage. Guinness can. Teddy bear. Various toys. Water pistol. Electric razor. Whistle
Wheelbarrow. *In it:* used can of paint, saucepan, jar containing trick snake, rubber hammer, colourful magazines **(Granny)**
Laundry tongs holding dirty nappy **(Slickerbotham)**
Sugar basin **(Freda)**
Aerosol labelled "Super Sterilizer" **(Clarissa)**
Glass milk jug **(Clarissa)**
Angler's net **(Freda)**

Personal: **Denis:** small bag of rubbish or apple, watch, very dirty handkerchief, packet of "Monster Munch", pickled onion

36 The Snatching of Horrible Harold

Edith: shopping bag. *In it:* packet of cream crackers
Granny Grot: *In her hat:* broccoli, rhubarb, celery and stick of liquorice. *In her pocket:* bag of "Grot Stoppers" spray of "Fleur de Grot" and conjurer's flower stick. *Up knicker leg:* bottle of "Grot Tonic" and till receipt roll
Mrs Thompson: newspaper and cigarette

ACT II

Strike: Wheelbarrow, coloured boxes

Set: Notice reading "Experiment A196 completed—Do Not Touch" over "After" exit on processor
In pram: paper and pencil, envelope, posters, plastic streamer can, cigar, syringe of Guinness. Notice on pram

Off stage: Duck weed, pond weed, old inner tube and old boot **(Slickerbotham, Clarissa and Freda)**
Earwigs and trick line by Zebra crossing
Cans of silly string and grottified cloths **(Slickerbotham, Clarissa and Freda)**
White laboratory table. *On it:* white sheet, microscope, large doctor's bag, huge axe, large mock syringe, saw, stethoscope (*bath shower attachment*), probe (*knitting needle*), brain scanner (*egg whisk*), huge magnifying glass, binoculars, pea (*Harold's brain*) microscope slide
Huge polystryene sandwich **(Denis)**
Baby's bottle full of Guinness **(Denis)**
Packet of cigarettes **(Denis)**
Toy spider—Wally **(Denis)**
Huge plastic bug **(Clarissa)**
Dandruff (Flaked rice) **Freda**

Personal: **Edith:** torch
Granny Grot: torch, telescope, anti-burglar poker, large felt-tip marker pen
Clarissa: stun spray (*aerosol*)
Freda: angler's net
Archie: large edible ham sandwich

NB At end of performance paint over keyhole shape drawn by Granny Grot

LIGHTING PLOT

ACT I

To open: Bright morning light

Cue 1	**Harold:** "Goody, goody!" *Blue flicker in pram*	(Page 2)
Cue 2	**Granny Grot:** "Silence please." *Dim lights*	(Page 7)
Cue 3	Door flies open *Lights up*	(Page 7)
Cue 4	**Granny Grot:** "Silence please." *Dim lights*	(Page 7)
Cue 5	Lid flies open *Lights up*	(Page 7)
Cue 6	**Granny Grot:** "Yes." *Lights fade on Granny Grot's and a cold blue light comes up on Slickerbotham's*	(Page 14)
Cue 7	As Processor starts up *Strobe lighting effect*	(Page 16)
Cue 8	They all exit into shop *House lights up*	(Page 18)

ACT II

To open: Evening

Cue 9	**Edith** and **Denis** exit *Fade lights and bring up ghostly blue light on Slickerbotham's shop*	(Page 21)
Cue 10	**Edith** and **Granny** exit *Fade to black-out*	(Page 24)
Cue 11	**Denis** enters *Bring lights slowly up*	(Page 24)
Cue 12	**Slickerbotham** and **assistants** enter with **Harold** in the pram *Bright green light over table*	(Page 24)
Cue 13	**Slickerbotham** looks into microscope *Dim lights*	(Page 26)
Cue 14	After tremulous chord *Lights up*	(Page 26)

Cue 15	**Denis** exits *Lights fade. Bring up dim light on Granny Grot's shop*	(Page 27)
Cue 16	**Granny, Edith** and **Denis** go into shop *Slowly bring up lights*	(Page 28)
Cue 17	As "After" door is opened *Light spot on Archie*	(Page 28)

EFFECTS PLOT

ACT I

The authors have given suggestions for suitable music effects (using the BBC range of Sound Effect records, which are available from Samuel French Ltd) but individual companies may well wish to select their own sound effects.

Cue 1	As play begins *"Street" music*	(Page 1)
Cue 2	As **Denis** throws rubbish into bin *Live drum roll and crash*	(Page 1)
Cue 3	**Denis:** "Now she tells me." *Loud music*	(Page 1)
Cue 4	**Mrs Thompson:** "... and his mum, Edith." *Music fades*	(Page 1)
Cue 5	**Denis** and **Mrs Thompson** (together): "Terrible business." *Loud music*	(Page 2)
Cue 6	**Edith:** "... tranny down a bit, love." *Music fades*	(Page 2)
Cue 7	**Harold:** "Goody, goody!" *Opening of "Play School" music*	(Page 2)
Cue 8	**Edith:** "...'e's on to Guinness, now." *Can being opened, poured and consumed. With loud burp?*	(Page 3)
Cue 9	**Denis:** "... boy and help your mum." *Music*	(Page 4)
Cue 10	As **Harold** enters Dry Cleaning Emporium *Fade music*	(Page 4)
Cue 11	**Slickerbotham** enters *Ghostly piano music. Low pitch version Side 2, track 4 from* Death and Horror	(Page 4)
Cue 12	**Denis:** "I ask you." *Hoovering, polishing and banging from Emporium*	(Page 5)
Cue 13	**Denis:** "... three bins full, Mr Slickerbotham." *Cue 12 sounds fade*	(Page 5)
Cue 14	**Slickerbotham** appears *Repeat Cue 11*	(Page 5)
Cue 15	**Slickerbotham** opens and closes door *Hoovering sounds fade in and fade out*	(Page 6)

Cue 16	**Denis:** ". . . go grananas when she sees. . ." *Bicycle bell, motor horn and train whistle (live)*	(Page 6)
Cue 17	**Granny** points at door a second time *Door flies open to magic sound—Side 1B, track 14 "Magic Mushroom" from* Out Of This World	(Page 7)
Cue 18	As chest flies open *Magic chord as Cue 17*	(Page 7)
Cue 19	**Denis** bangs his head *Motor horn*	(Page 8)
Cue 20	**Granny:** "Yes—how?" *Crashes and bangs from Emporium*	(Page 11)
Cue 21	**Slickerbotham:** "Oh, shut up!" *Sad music—Side 2, track 5 "Kittens Lullaby" from* Radiophonic Workshop	(Page 12)
Cue 22	**Edith:** ". . . to love Harold like me." *Music fades*	(Page 13)
Cue 23	**Slickerbotham** enters *Great Dictator music. Side 1, track 28, "Minds of Evil" from* Radiophonic Workshop 21	(Page 14)
Cue 24	**Megagerm** enters *Side 1, track 14, "The Chem Lab Mystery" from* Radiophonic Workshop 21	(Page 16)
Cue 25	**Clarissa:** "Confirmed." *Sound of the Processor. Side 2, band 2, track 15, "Dr Jekyll's Lab" from* Death and Horror	(Page 16)
Cue 26	**Slickerbotham:** "Shut up!" *Loud noises as per script*	(Page 17)
Cue 27	**Slickerbotham:** "ONE! Open!" *Sounds stop*	(Page 17)
Cue 28	**Freda** and **Clarissa:** "Aye. There's the rub!" *Side 1, band 28, "Minds of Evil" from* Radiophonic Workshop 21	(Page 18)

ACT II

Cue 29	As Curtain rises *Dog barking, cat meowing*	(Page 19)
Cue 30	As Lights fade *Spooky music. Side 1, track 1, "Quatermass and the Pit" from* Radiophonic Workshop 21	(Page 19)
Cue 31	**Freda and Clarissa:** "Earwigs!" *Earwig music*	(Page 22)
Cue 32	Lights fade to Black-out *Sinister music. Side 2, track 4, "Mysterioso", from* Radiophonic Workshop 21	(Page 24)

The Snatching of Horrible Harold 41

Cue 33	**Slickerbotham:** "Hurry. Hurry." *Loud bumping noises*	(Page 24)
Cue 34	**Freda and Clarissa:** ". . . and pulse rate." *Short snatch of loud music*	(Page 25)
Cue 35	As Lights dim *Tremulous single chord*	(Page 26)
Cue 36	**Edith** and **Granny** enter *Side 1, track 22, "Secrets of the Chasm", from* Radiophonic Workshop 21	(Page 27)
Cue 37	**Edith** and **Granny** walk up the street *Glockenspiel on each step they take*	(Page 27)
Cue 38	**Granny** opens door *Side 1B, track 14, "Magic Mushroom", from* Out Of This World	(Page 27)
Cue 39	**Granny:** "Quick, into the shop." *Side 1, track 22, "Secrets of the Chasm", from* Radiophonic Workshop 21	(Page 28)
Cue 40	**Granny** puts telescope to Archie's chest *Side 1, track 2, "Colonel Bloodnok's Stomach" from* Radiophonic Workshop 21	(Page 28)
Cue 41	**Granny:** "Right, here goes." *Processor sounds. Side 2, track 2, no. 15, "Dr Jekyll's Lab", from* Death and Horror	(Page 29)
Cue 42	**Edith:** ". . . delicate as Harold." *Sounds stop*	(Page 29)
Cue 43	**Harold:** "Gotcher". *Repeat Cue 41*	(Page 31)
Cue 44	**Granny:** "Why not!" *Louder Processor sounds*	(Page 32)
Cue 45	**Archie:** "Open the door, Denis." *Sounds stop*	(Page 32)
Cue 46	**Harold:** "Not likely!" *Loud music*	(Page 33)
Cue 47	**Granny:** " . . . really something." *Music stops*	(Page 33)
Cue 48	Finale music *Side 2, band 2, "The Broken Biscuit Club", from* Radiophonic Workshop 21	(Page 33)

Sound Effect Record List

Out of this World—BBC Records REC 225 Stereo
Death and Horror—BBC Records REC 269 Stereo
Radiophonic Workshop—BBC Records REC 196 Stereo
Radiophonic Workshop '21—BBC Records REC 354 Stereo.

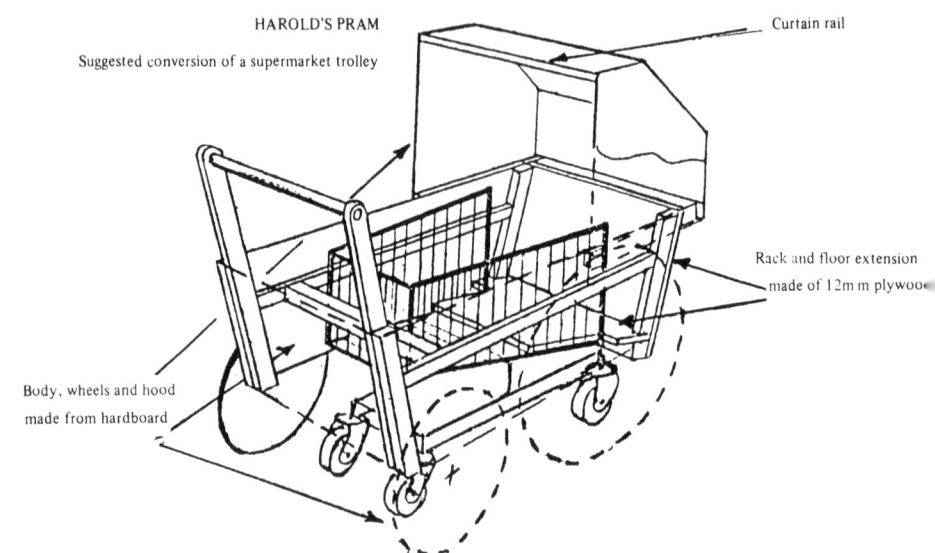

MADE AND PRINTED IN GREAT BRITAIN BY
LATIMER TREND & COMPANY LTD, PLYMOUTH
MADE IN ENGLAND